TOOLBOX
FOR
EVANGELISM

Basic Christian Principles to Help You Share the Faith

BRADY COOK

BRADY COOK

Toolbox for Evangelism

Contents

Dedication

To Africa, who taught me what it meant to love something eternal

After This Book...

Thank you for buying my book! It is my genuine and prayerful hope that you will grow from the material contained within these pages, and that you will revisit it often whenever you find yourself wanting to draw closer to God (which hopefully will be often!).

As a way for me to further say "thank you," there is a special offer at the back end of this book that I hope you'll enjoy. It is absolutely free, and designed to help you grow in your faith as well, just like this book. Thanks again!

In Him,
Brady Cook

Why the Need for This Book?

"And they said, "Come, let us build for ourselves a city, and a tower whose top will reach into heaven, and let us make for ourselves a name; lest we be scattered abroad over the face of the whole earth." And the Lord came down to see the city and the tower which the sons of men had built. And the Lord said, "Behold, they are one people, and they all have the same language. And this is what they began to do, and now nothing which they purpose to do will be impossible for them." (**Genesis 11:4-6**)

Evangelism. That one word sums up what we do, who we are, why we live, how we talk, and everything else that makes up who are as Christians. Because of that, It is by far the most talked about subject in churches, not just in today's time, but since the beginning of Jesus' ministry. And it is a uniquely Christian concept. The Jews were not heavily evangelistic (although Matthew 23:15 does discuss proselytizing), and other religions seek to entice by other avenues. The social gospel aims at your belly, Christian-themed rock concerts shoot for your emotions, debates aim at your mind, but only the pure Gospel of Jesus Christ is the one that seeks to engage your soul.

It might seem weird then to begin a class on evangelism with a seemingly "minor" story from the Old Testament, one in which the world does not appear to do anything "wrong" per se, but nevertheless God decides to intervene. Seeing that the world operates as one, and that through their unity, "nothing will be impossible for them," God decides to confuse their language and "scatter them over the face of the earth." A somewhat anti-type to this is found in Acts 2, where the Holy Spirit descends on the Apostles and allows them to speak in tongues, so that everyone "heard them in their own language that they were born" (Acts 2:8). And what was it that the Apostles were talking about? You guessed it, the Good News of Jesus Christ. So, in a way, one can imagine that the work of the Gospel and spreading it to all corners of the world is a continuation of what we find in Genesis 11, trying to find our brothers and sisters that were scattered, and uniting them under the banner of the Cross.

1

What is Evangelism?

With the myriad of classes/workshops/sermons/books/etc that exist on the topic, one would think that practicing evangelism is tantamount to climbing Mt. Everest barefoot with a 300 pound baboon strapped to their back. In reality, all it is is simply telling people about the Gospel. We get bogged down thinking that our main agenda is to get people baptized, and not just one, but 100's every week; if we don't, we're letting God down. Such is just simply not the case. Remember, God isn't asking you to twist people's arm and force a conversion that isn't there, He's simply asking us to talk to other people about obeying God (Matt. 28:16-20).

Romans 10:14 puts it in simpler terms: "How then shall they call upon Him in whom they have not believed? And how shall they believe in Him whom they have not heard? And how shall they hear without a preacher?" The "preacher" in that phrase is not describing someone who gets up in a suit every Sunday and talks for exactly 32.5 minutes, but rather us as Christians; the duty falls on all of us. As a matter of fact, evangelism operates off of three basic tenets: (1) everyone can do it, (2) everyone needs to do it, and (3) everyone should be doing it all the time.

All it takes is a basic understanding of the Gospel, and a genuine concern for other people's souls. And before you wonder if you have that "basic understanding of the Gospel," ask yourself, "Am I a Christian?" If so, you know at least enough for what you needed to do; that's enough to get started.

What we miss in the big scheme of the New Testament is the relative lack of education amongst early Christians. We read their letters and see their testimony and think, "these must have been people of amazing understanding!" Yet Acts 4:13 tells quite a different story. There, the Jewish authorities marveled at the understanding of Peter and John, and, knowing that they were nothing more than everyday fishermen, concluded that they had to have "been with Jesus." Sure, they had sat at the feet of the Messiah for over three full years, hearing His words and seeing His miracles, but we can do the same with a thorough reading of the New Testament.

Consider also the example of the blind man in John 9. Here, we have the example of a man that is "blind from birth" (John 9:1). He probably did not enjoy a first-class education at the finest yeshivas in the land, but his discourse with the Pharisees reveals an understanding of God far above those who had spent their entire life in the Law. Those men had their own disagreement as to the nature of Jesus (John 9:16), but when they asked the blind man his opinion in verse 17, he simply replied, "He is a prophet," and by the time you get to verse 34, they accuse him of trying to teach them something about the Law! What's the point here then? That you have to have some kind of great theological understanding of all the nuances of Biblical understanding to teach the Gospel? Quite the opposite: that anyone, anytime, anywhere has the ability to teach another person the word of God.

One last example. In Mark 5:1-20 (and Luke 8:26-39), the story is told of a demon-possessed man that is cured by Jesus. Afterwards, he was "entreating" Jesus to follow Him everywhere. Normally, this would signal to us the perfect type of convert, but Jesus turns him around, and tells him to "go home" and "report to them what great things the Lord has done for you, and how He had mercy on you." Has the Lord done great things for you? Has He given you a hope of salvation? Go home and tell people about it!

2

Top Ten Misunderstood Things About Evangelism

With the perception that Evangelism is some kind of mystical/optional concept, comes some very easily misunderstood things in regards to it, and if we were honest with ourselves, it is often times these misunderstandings that keeps us from practicing evangelism. Clearing some of these things up will help us to be the kind of active disciple that we should be.

1. **Evangelism is not a "technique" (1 Corinthians 1:18-20; 2:1-2)** - Calling it a "technique" implies a lack of authenticity, where conversions occur as a result of our skill rather than the Gospel. Can different methods be learned? Absolutely. Should we rely on our own abilities instead of God? Never.
2. **Evangelism is not optional (Matthew 28:16-20)** - Evangelism should not be something that's relegated to a chosen few, or the "super-Christians;" we should all be active in evangelism. Remember, it's called "the Great Commandment," not "the Great Suggestion."

3. **Evangelism is not solely example-based (1 Peter 2:11-12)** - We have all heard that old song that "you may be the only Bible this world ever reads." While that's true, sitting around and waiting for someone to recognize your holiness is a recipe for disaster. Example-based evangelism should be in addition to active evangelism, not an excuse for laziness.

4. **Evangelism is not only about baptism (1 Corinthians 1:15-17)** - Baptism for the remission of sins is an essential part of salvation, but it is not the *only* step in the process. Getting the person to a point of faith and confession is necessary as well, or baptism becomes nothing more than a very public bath.

5. **Evangelism is not all about attendance (Hebrews 10:24-25)** - The mark of a sound Christian includes faithful attendance with the saints, but attendance cannot mask an unrighteous life. If our goal in conversion is simply to get them at services every week, then we've missed the point.

6. **Evangelism is not only logic-based (1 Corinthians 11:17-34)** - If intellect alone were all that was needed for someone to convert to Christ, then Bibles air-dropped from the sky would be a valuable evangelistic tool. Unfortunately, emotions also play a big role, and we need to be ready to address those as well.

7. **Evangelism is not effortless (Acts 26:27-29)** - One look in the pages of our Bible, and it becomes evident very quickly how much labor went into spreading the first-century church. Shame on us for believing that we're entitled to a fraction of their blood, sweat, and tears.

8. **Evangelism is not usually comfortable (2 Corinthians**

11:16-33) - Trying to change the heart of a person requires constant exploration of God's Word, turning over stones in a person several times to uncover the true roots of disobedience. This will most likely not be a pleasant time for anyone, but it will be oh-so-worth-it.

9. **Evangelism is not a one-conversation proposition (John 21:15-17; Acts 20:28-31)** - Can anyone be converted in a matter of minutes or hours like the Ethiopian Eunich was (Acts 8)? Sure, but most of the time it requires a regular and ongoing conversation. Don't be discouraged when they're not baptized in the first 20 minutes.

10. **Evangelism is not only based in a church building (John 4:1-24; Acts 16:13-15)** - We have to get past the idea that conversions only occur as a result of a rousing sermon that convicts the soul and storms the will; those still happen, but they are by no means the only place conversions occur. Do not discount dinner-table conversations and coffee-shop evangelism in your quest to save souls.

3

Recognizing the Need

Grace is something that we as Christians rightfully understand, but sometimes do not appreciate. Without an active prayer and study life, God's mercy that was extended towards us can become old news; unfortunately, that also extends to a lackadaisical evangelistic effort. If we are truly to be pleasing to Him, the fact that we are forgiven sinners must remain forefront in our mind, and the desire to extend that mercy to others must be the motivation behind why we tell them about the Gospel in the first place. People that leave the faith often do so because, somewhere along the way, they forgot how great a gift it is. That's where we come in.

We have already stated (and will continue to state) that evangelism is a pressing need for all Christians to participate in, but up until this point, the emphasis has been largely on it as a command. That is a good place to start from, but very quickly in our lives it should develop into a fervent desire on our behalf to want to see other people be saved. Consider the conversation that Jesus had with His disciples before the feeding of the 5,000: they recognized the need for food to be supplied for the masses (Mark 6:35-36), but believed it was "their problem, not ours."

Jesus, who had "compassion for them, because they were like sheep without a shepherd" (Mark 6:34), tells them to solve it, which Jesus does through the intervention of a miracle. But the point is made: when you see your brother in need, do what you can to help (1 John 3:17; James 2:15-16), especially if they are a Christian (Galatians 6:10). When this real need is seen and considered, then evangelism isn't a chore, anymore than rescuing a drowning child out of a lake would be. Of course, you'll have to get up out of your chair and gets your clothes drenched, but wouldn't you be willing to make that sacrifice to save someone's life?! It's the same with evangelism.

At this point, you may be saying, "yea, let's do it!" But the sad reality of all of this is that we see needs everyday and fail to act on them, and I don't just mean Jim-the-water-cooler guy either, I mean people that we pass in the trailer parks and "on the other side of the tracks." Do we write people off because of the perception that we have towards them (James 2:1-5)? I've made this mistake as much as anyone, and only by realizing it can we do anything about it.

When people walk into our building, the setting and candidate are perfect for evangelism; it's when we go outside the walls that we run into trouble. Besides, no one is watching your every move to see if you're telling people about the Gospel, so the chances are small that anyone will take you to task for it. But ask yourself, what if I was judged on my evangelism efforts as I was my baptism? How does my obedience to "doctrine" stack up to my love for others? The visible things are easily taken care of, it's matters of the heart that we have to sheriff ourselves.

There are two types of lost people: those that have never

heard the Gospel, ad those that have fallen away from the Truth. Both need the Gospel, even if the approach is different.

4

Creating a Culture

Many churches talk about evangelism, but few ever put it into practice. A lot of good ideas, and even better intentions, but often it is put on the back burner in favor of "more pressing issues." Because it's hard, and also, because the amount of success you have isn't reflected in the amount of work you do, no one holds anybody else accountable. "Evangelism" efforts are usually relegated to "having a good influence" and hoping people will come to God based on your example, which is good, but not quite what God is after (Matt. 10:33). How do we change that?

In Acts 17, Paul and company arrive in Thessalonica, and, as was their custom, they ventured into the synagogue and began to teach. And, as commonly occurred during those times, many people believed in Jesus as a result – Jews, as well as "a great multitude of the God-fearing Greeks and a number of leading women." This obviously upset the ones who cared greatly about their social and financial standing, and so a riot ensued, dragging innocent Christians before the city authorities. Their charge? "These men who have upset the world have come here also" (Acts 17:6). What a compliment!

Would to God that Greenville would say of Hillside, that we have "turned the world upside down" with the teaching of God! It is possible, but it does not happen by accident. It takes creating an environment where evangelism is encouraged and expected by everyone.

> *Is evangelism a part of your church's DNA? Is it commonly understood – and expected – that each individual member will invite and study with people on their own? Or is it one of those things that people must be forced to do, usually against their will?*

Sometimes it takes a special "event" to get a church kickstarted in the right direction. And, before you burn this book (and my house) to the ground, what I don't mean is an "event" with moonbounces and hot-dogs; those superficial and unScriptural ideas do nothing but convince the world that the Gospel is not enough. What I mean by "event" are things such as a special sermon geared around reaching those that are outside. Preaching on the "thief on the cross?" That's always a hot-button issue, and it makes sense to use those opportunities to make a special effort to invite friends. Having a Gospel Meeting that's themed around a unique issue (mormonism, islam, authority, etc)? Encourage other members to really make a push to invite outsiders into the assembly. The more focused opportunities we can provide to teach people the Gospel, the more we can reach specific people that are dealing with specific issues.

Another effective (albeit more obvious) way to create this "culture of evangelism" is to celebrate evangelism that's already taken place (Luke 15:7). Has someone recently been

11

converted? Discuss it. Are there those present that need to be? Talk to them about it. The more it is on the forefront of our minds, the more it will be on the forefront of our hearts.

I have also seen churches that task a small group of people to focus heavily on evangelism for a certain time period (usually one week to a month), and report to the church on what they've done (1 Corinthians 3:6); after that, a new group will form. This not only creates an air of accountability within those group members, but also exposes the rest of the congregation to the potentiality of a focused, unified approach.

Without a doubt, the best way to kickstart a church into an evangelistic mindset is by focusing on what you do as an individual first; after all, if you're not participating in it yourself, no one else has a reason to be. By modeling an evangelistic effort, you will encourage other people to do the same, and if enough people take it upon themselves, the church will literally transform in front of our eyes.

A church that has a "culture of evangelism" is a church where evangelism is: preached on, encouraged by the leadership, held accountable by the flock, and valued by the individual.

5

What We Can Expect

The understatement of the year goes to Jesus in John 16:33, when He spoke to His Apostles before facing His own crucifixion: "In the world you have tribulation, but take courage; I have overcome the world." That statement is loaded on both sides, first, because Christ overcame the world in a myriad of ways, but secondly, to say that we will face opposition in the world is a well-known fact. Jesus taught it, the apostles experienced it, and so we can expect it.

> *Bible reading and studying are important, but eventually the time will come when we have to get out and confront someone who disagrees with us. Anytime we do that, it's bound to get a little bit interesting.*

Understanding the realities of what we will face is not pessimism; it's the key to effective preparation. We get caught up in the numbers of passages like Acts 2, where Luke records that 3,000 souls were converted! What we overlook sometimes is that scholars estimate that the number of Jews present in Jerusalem at the time would have been anywhere from 1-3 million people. Somehow, from that angle, 3,000 people doesn't really sound like a lot. And while Paul and his companions went about preaching and teaching in all these different cities, we have to remember that many of those converts were Jews that saw Jesus as a fulfillment of the Gospel, as well as gentiles who had never heard about this Yeshua of Nazareth before. Today is quite different. Not only have people heard about Jesus, but their opinions about Him are so firmly set in stone that it is hard to convince them of anything different. Not impossible, but surely more difficult.

It would do us well sometimes to temper our expectations in regards to the Gospel. While it would be nice if every single person we talked to was receptive, the truth is that hardly any will. But even at that, all the hostilities, the refusals, and the hateful words will be worth it if we can bring even one soul to Christ.

"I alone am left; and they seek my life, to take it away."
(1 Kings 19:10)

The persecution that we will inevitably face notwithstanding, the hardest battles that we will face is with people who are stubbornly resistant to change. We will encounter people that are on their 3rd (or more!) marriage, as well as people that refuse to admit doctrinal error, even when the Scriptures plainly disagree with them. Others will be reluctant for a more emotional reason; maybe a close family member was steeped in error, and so their conversion would be tantamount to an acceptance of their condemnation. In those instances, the words of the rich man from Luke 16 would be applicable: "He said, 'Then I beg you, Father, that you send him to my father's house — for I have five brothers — that he may warn them, lest they also come to this place of torment." It's not our place to judge someone's eternal location, except as outlined throughout Scripture, but if it is in fact true that their place is not in Heaven, the one thing they want their loved ones that are still living to understand is to do everything possible to avoid torment.

Jesus' words about persecution are just as true in today's world as they were 2,000 years ago, but that doesn't in any way negate the command we have to teach other people the Gospel.

Hard Facts We Would Do Well to Remember:
1. **Most people are not interested in the truth (Matthew 7:13-14)**
2. **Many people we teach will not respond (John 6:60-66)**
3. **We are not responsible to force conversion on our neighbors (only teach) (1 Corinthians 3:5-7)**
4. **We must fulfill our mission (2 Peter 2:5)**

6

Turning the Conversation

Picture yourself on an average workday. You walk into your cubicle/office on Monday morning, say hello to the guys around you, and plop down in your chair. Rick, the guy next to you who insists on playing his 80's rock a little too high, leans around the corner and begins talking to you about the game yesterday, how his fantasy team is awful, and how he can't wait until lunch time because he wants to try that new burger place downtown. After about five minutes of small talk, he goes back to work and you turn back around to your computer. Simple enough, right? But here's the million dollar question: did you just miss an opportunity to evangelize?

Your specific story may vary from that (slightly), but the fact is exactly the same: we miss opportunities all day long simply because we fail to recognize them. In John 4, after Jesus has just completed a fantastic theological conversation with the woman at the well, his disciples come to Him astonished, not at the reception of the woman, but that He had been talking to her in the first place (John 4:27)! First off, she was a woman - which was indefensible by itself - and secondly, she was a samaritan! Why would Jesus have wasted His precious time with such a "lowlife" as her! Jesus responds to this mentality with a profound teaching on looking past the immediate: "Do you not say, 'There are yet four months, and then comes the harvest'? Behold, I say to you, lift up your eyes, and look on the fields, that they are white for harvest" (John 4:35). Chances are, every single one of the Apostles would have by-passed the woman, relegating her to second class citizenship and unworthy of the Gospel, but Jesus did not, and His teaching in verse 35 emphasizes that sometimes we overlook opportunities that are staring us right in the face. The list of times that Jesus did this could go on and on: Zaccheus (Luke 19), the blind man (John 9), the adulterous woman (John 8), to name a few. All opportunities, but more than likely missed by the majority of Christians.

> *What are some missed opportunities that you can re-member in the past year? The past month? The past week?*

No one is immune to this by the way. Everyone misses potential conversions, the Apostles just happened to be the easiest targets. So this begs the question, how do we turn these regular opportunities into potential Bible discussions?

1. Look for openings in the conversation.
2. Start where they are.
3. Talk to them about obedience.
4. Invite them to services.
5. Close the conversation

> *There's no such thing as a "perfect opening" or a "fool-*

proof study plan"; everything revolves around listening to what they have to say, considering their knowledge, and bringing it back to the Bible.

7

The Power of Questions

If the candidate and the setting were perfect 100% of the time, none of us would have any anxiety when it comes to teaching others. They would sincerely ask questions seeking Bible truth, and we, in response, would shower them with our vast knowledge. Unfortunately what happens far too often is a question will pop up that we are unprepared for, and we'll stammer through an answer as best we know how, which might or might not be satisfactory to the hearer. Spending the next 80 years in self-reflective study notwithstanding, is there a better way to respond? How about answering their question with a question?

Many of us have never tried nor thought of this avenue before, simply because we're too caught up in wanting to have the answer to everything ten years before they ask. But by asking a question in response to their query, it removes the hostility from the conversation, and forces them to answer and think for themselves.

Answering a question with a question puts the ball back in their court, and allows the conversation to continue on their terms.

Jesus was no stranger to the "question with a question" mentality (Jewish rabbis today still use this method, called Pilpul).
While He could have very easily answered any one of their
concerns/complaints with minimal effort, He chose to respond
in a way that allowed them to see the answer for themselves.
Consider the following responses from Jesus:

- Mark 10:17-18: "And as He was setting out on a journey, a
  man ran up to Him and knelt before Him, and began asking
  Him, 'Good Teacher, what shall I do to inherit eternal life?'
  And Jesus said to him, 'Why do you call Me good?'"
- Matthew 22:17-20: "Tell us therefore, what do You think?
  Is it lawful to give a poll-tax to Caesar, or not?"... And they
  brought Him a denarius. And He said to them, 'Whose
  likeness and inscription is this?'"
- Matthew 12:10-11: "And they questioned Him, saying, 'Is it
  lawful to heal on the Sabbath?' — in order that they might
  accuse Him. And He said to them, 'What man shall there
  be among you, who shall have one sheep, and if it falls into
  a pit on the Sabbath, will he not take hold of it, and lift it
  out?'"

Jesus was a master at this type of response. The Scriptures are
replete with the fact that many of these questions that were
posed to Him were intended to "trap" or "ensnare" Him; by
putting the onus of the question back on them, they were the
ones that were forced to agree or disagree with God instead.
People today do the exact same thing. When they ask us, "Why
do you believe in God?" do you honestly believe that they are
interested in hearing our answer? Some may, but by and large

many times they are trying to get us to question our faith. By responding with something along the lines of "Why do you not?" it forces them to evaluate their own lack of faith as opposed to my belief. In evaluating this type of thinking, C.S. Lewis once said: "If you are a Christian, you don't have to believe that all the other religions are simply wrong though. If you are an atheist, you do have to believe that the main point in all the religions of the whole world is simply one huge mistake."

To be fair, sometimes answering a question with a direct answer is the preferable route. When Jesus was asked "Which commandment is foremost of all?" Jesus answered with a definitive, direct answer (Mark 12:28-31). But often, questions can be answered by inviting the questioner to think for themselves.

8

The Power of Parables

Rightly did Jesus quote from the prophet Isaiah when He spoke in Matthew 15:8: "This people honors Me with their lips, but their heart is far from Me" (Mark 7:6; Isaiah 29:13). The insistence of the religious leaders of the day to put their own traditions ahead of the commandments of God had left the people of that day feeling a sense of disconnectedness from their God - not unlike what many people today feel. While we are very good at taking people to various passages to show them Biblical truths, I would argue that the main problem many people have with God is not a logical understanding of His Gospel, but an emotional one. We have not allowed the facts of the Gospel to pierce our own hearts, and so we can't help them to pierce others' also (Matthew 13:10-17).

This is why Jesus went around teaching in parables (Matthew 13:34; Mark 4:34). A parable is nothing more than a simple story designed to teach a great theological truth: a man sowing some seed (evangelism), a man mugged and left for dead (compassion), a woman that wears down a judge (persistence in prayer), a generous landowner who rewards his laborers equally (grace), and a father who loses a son, and eagerly awaits his return (forgiveness).

It is one thing to try to talk to people about these concepts, but it is quite another to teach them in such a way as to have them pierce the heart of the listener. So effective was Jesus' use of parables, that when soldiers were sent to arrest him and bring him back to the pharisees, the men went back empty-handed, saying, "Never did a man speak the way this man speaks" (John 7:46).

It helps Jesus' creative juices that He is the Son of God, but that does not mean that any of us are incapable of telling other people God's truths by similar methods. Like the people of Jesus' day, many of our contacts will not be the theologically elite, but common laborers and workmen who are simply interested in drawing closer to Him. Many of the answers that they have gotten from their "pastors" and other spiritual leaders probably have them feeling the same way that many of Jesus' audience did, and so bringing the story of the cross back down to its elementary level is the first step in reaching their hearts (1 Corinthians 2:2).

Parables - like the one that Nathan used in 2 Samuel 12 - allow the hearer to issue judgment based on a 3rd person perspective - what they would do if they were them. Because of this, they remain an effective tool in helping an otherwise obstinate person see their own condition. The next time you encounter someone that seems bent on never changing their perspective or attitude, try approaching them with an illustration of some kind instead; their response may shock you.

9

What About Our Visitors?

In a perfect world, people would walk into our building on Sundays or Wednesdays, and the only thing they would care about is whether or not the teaching is sound and the worship is Biblical. The extraneous things, such as the clock that has stopped working, the carpets that are ripped, and the endless amounts of non-worship related papers strewn all the pews would not bother them at all. Unfortunately, reality is quite the opposite. When visitors walk into our assembly, they will immediately notice some very physical things, and the way they are perceived will tell that individual a lot about how we view God. Is the building a mess? Do some of the bulbs need to be changed? Is the bathroom trash overflowing? Then it would seem these people must not care very much about their God (1 Corinthians 14:23).

> *"Do not neglect to show hospitality to strangers, for by this some have entertained angels without knowing it."* (Hebrews 13:2)

One of the main things that will be perceived is our enthusiasm and love for one another. If someone walks in and takes their seat, and it is ten minutes before they are greeted, that's something they will notice. They'll also notice if the members have zero interest in even talking to each other. In short, after we've done all the hard work of inviting and encouraging someone to come and visit our congregation, we can not afford to drop the ball at the goal line when someone actually takes the time and effort to come into our assembly.

The truth is though, this is something we instinctively know. All of us, at one point or another, have walked into a business, or even visited another church, where no one made the effort to even acknowledge your existence. How did that make you feel? Did you, for better or for worse, make a snap decision as to the state of that Church? Would you ever want to visit again? Imagine how a visitor for our services would feel. This is someone who is in a completely vulnerable position, doesn't know many people, may not be familiar with Biblical worship, and is probably afraid of sitting in someone's seat! It's our job to make them feel welcome.

> *"And be kind to one another, tender-hearted, forgiving each other, just as God in Christ also has forgiven you."*
> *(Ephesians 4:32)*

Often times, its the little things that will help. If you see someone new in the parking lot, instead of ignoring them, walk up and engage them in conversation before you even walk in the building. Then, once you're inside the building, introduce them to other members. Ask about their kids (or grandkids), where they work at, what area of town they live in, what brings them to our congregation - anything that makes them feel welcome.

A positive, smiling face can go a long way in making them feel comfortable worshipping there. As Paul said, "I became all things to all men, so that I might, by all means, save some" (1 Corinthians 9:22). Then, once the assembly begins, focus on the worship, showing them that you're vested in what you're doing. Nothing is more awkward then worshipping God with a bunch of people who don't look like they want to be there either.

Visitor's brochures, business cards, Bible class material, all of those are physical things that you and I can hand out to people as they walk in to help them be more familiar with who we are. But what about after they leave? Fortunately, we have the visitor's cards that are passed out and collected after every service; make a special effort to utilize those. Call or write a quick note to let them know you appreciate them coming, and ask if there would be a time that they would be willing to study. Following up and making contact on more than just the first visit will help initiate a second. There is a line that can be crossed in this (which is called harassment), but no one has ever complained that a church was "too nice." Imagine how you would feel if everyone at a church wrote you a card after a visit!

10

No One is Unreachable

It's hard for us to imagine now, but there once was a time when Paul the Apostle was thought of as being "unreachable." A "hebrew of hebrews" as he calls himself (Philippians 3:5), there was no one who was more zealous, more anti-Christ than Paul. And yet, as he describes later, he was "shown mercy, because he did it ignorantly in unbelief" (1 Timothy 1:13).

> *What would you do if you saw someone that (you thought) had absolutely zero chance of becoming a Christian? Would you still take the time to teach them?*

The reputation against Paul was so bad, that, after his conversion, when Paul tried to associate with the disciples in Jerusalem, they wouldn't have anything to do with him (Acts 9:26); it took the intervention of Barnabas to convince them otherwise. Later, Paul would write about the incredulity of this conversion when he would write to Timothy: "It is a trustworthy statement, deserving full acceptance, that Christ Jesus came into the world to save sinners, among whom I am foremost of all. And yet for this reason I found mercy, in order that in me as the foremost, Jesus Christ might demonstrate His perfect patience, as an example for those who would believe in Him for eternal life" (1 Tim. 1:16-17). Notice especially that second verse: one of the reasons that Paul was "shown mercy" was so that other people could look at his example and say, "if he can be forgiven, so can I."

That being said, how many times have we written off people and said to ourselves, "they will never become a Christian," and move on about our day. And yet, they very well could if someone would give them a chance. Am I willing?

Generally speaking, the ones that we think are the hardest to reach are the ones whose sin is heavily intertwined with their lifestyle: bar owners, prostitutes, drug addicts, and, even though it's not the same as the other things, those who are in unscriptural marriages. It's bad enough to meet someone who has multiple difficulties, but can you imagine meeting someone who has multiple?! And yet, when Jesus approached Sychar, a city of Samaria, that's exactly what He found. John 4 tells the story of a woman who was just about as steeped in immorality as could possibly be found, and yet, Jesus was able to reach her. Consider all He had working against Him in this encounter:

- **Socio-Economic Difficulties:** Not only was this person a samaritan, but a woman at that (John 4:9, 27)! It would've been awkward for Jewish and Samaritan men to be talking, much less a man and woman!
- **Poor Home Life:** Verses 16-18 bring her position into full view: five husbands and the one she has now she isn't even married to! Imagine encountering that!
- **Uncomfortable Setting:** As if Jesus' task of talking to a samaritan woman wasn't hard enough, can you fathom doing it on her turf without a support system! (John 4:8)

- **Worship Issues:** Hard to convert someone because they're the music minster at a congregation? Imagine trying to convert someone who was a samaritan!

Now, are these types of situations hard? Absolutely. But are they impossible? Absolutely not. Chances are, 99 out of 100 people you would talk to in situations like these will never obey the Gospel, but let that be their decision. As was mentioned before, our job is not to force people to obey against their will, but to simply tell them the Gospel. Let us never be guilty of pre-judging anyone as "unworthy" of the love of God. Tell people the Word, and let them decide for themselves.

11

Where Did All the Churches Go?

It's an all-too-familiar story: new work starts in a new location, members stir up excitement and growth begins to take place. Visitors come every week, contacts are made, and conversions are frequent. Over time though, that congregation that was initially started with such great energy has begun to slip away, and only a few members are left of what was a once great church in the community. Refusing to give up, they are forced off the property, whether through financial, personal, or spiritual reasons. Another beacon gone.

A similar story is told in the first few chapters of the book of Samuel. After so much enthusiasm surrounding the completion of Solomon's Temple (1 Kings 8), the nation begins to fall into a state of spiritual decay. The people have gone so far from God, that when Hannah arrives to bemoan her infertility, Eli the Priest believes that she is drunk (1 Samuel 1:12-14). What does that say about the commitment of the Jews?! Consider the great response in Jerusalem on the day of Pentecost (Acts 2:37-41); now, how big is that congregation? It's not uncommon for churches to die, but shame on some for letting it happen!

Remember: A church that grows by economics, will die by economics. Translation? If you're relying on booming industries in your town to drive church growth, the inverse will become true if/when those businesses leave town. Sound evangelistic practices thrive in spite of local economics.

Another sad example is shown by the nation of Israel in Judges 2:7-11. After their triumphant declaration in Joshua 24 that they will only serve the Lord (Joshua 24:16-18), Judges 2;10 declares that a generation arose that did not "know the Lord, nor yet the work which He had done for Israel." Because of their failure to train the next generation (Deuteronomy 6:20-25), a nation of Israel reached adulthood that had no knowledge of where they had come from, and more importantly, no appreciation for what God had done for them. This happens in congregations today all the time. A failure of sound, fundamental Bible teaching in children's classes, and a lack of Biblical instruction at home, leads to a generation that cares nothing for God.

These, among other things, are the problems that we should seek to avoid. Too often we have seen kids leave sound churches for denominations, simply because they are "more fun;" that should never be the litmus test for a congregation. The list that follows states more items that we would do well to avoid.

How to Kill a Church:
1. Failure to practice evangelism.
2. Lack of Biblical leadership.
3. Aim to maintain.
4. Members don't care about each other.

5. Avoid issues within the church.
6. Ignore the young people.

12

When to Talk About Hell

While it's true that Jesus spoke more about Hell than He did Heaven, we must understand that He did it for a specific point: because there would be some that would not follow Him based on a love for God, but rather out of a desire to avoid Hell. That type of thinking is infantile, and must change with the growth of the individual Christian, but it is not a bad starting point to begin with some people. Jesus mentioned the pain of hell three times in His "mutilation discourse" (Mark 9:43-48), and if it takes that fear to follow God from time to time, so be it. But is it proper to bring it up during the first conversation we have with a new convert?

The answer is both yes and no. While it is necessary sometimes to discuss hellfire as a Biblical reality, a morbid desire to "scare" people is never appropriate. Anytime a discussion of impending torment is applicable, it should always be done in a sense of genuine love and a desire to see that person avoid it. While God is the God of justice and punishment, He is also the God of mercy, love and reconciliation. Those are some of the attributes we need to be trumpeting about Him as well.

Just as important as "when" Jesus talked about Hell is "how;"

the context surrounding when He invoked that fear is a good guideline for us to use. For instance, the references used Matthew 13:38-42, 22:13, and 25:28-30, all have to do with an "inclusion" approach. In other words, there are those that will be a part of God's people, and there are those who are not, and the key is to make sure that you are part of the right group! In that sense, helping people to understand that Hell is not a place where God sends you, but rather where you send yourself, will help them to understand the true nature of God's judgment, as well as the steps necessary to avoid it.

> *I don't respect people who don't proselytize. If you believe there is a Heaven and a Hell and people could be going to Hell ... and you think it's not worth telling them this because it would make it socially awkward ... how much do you have to hate someone to not proselytize? How much do you have to hate someone to believe everlasting life is possible and not tell them that?" - Penn Jillette*

Any discussion about Hell has to eventually revolve around an understanding about what sin is (Isaiah 59:1-2). Once that is in place, then Hell becomes a certainty, instead of this mystical place that most pretend doesn't exist. After it becomes a certainty, it is understandable that most would want to avoid it; vis-a-vis, understand sin, obey God, and avoid Hell. That is the rubric for a more "logical" conversion. It's when emotion moves into the picture that the case must be made more firm that this is a place you definitely want to avoid.

Hell should drive our motivation but not our conversation; unnecessary fear-mongering and scare tactics have no place in a Biblically sound Bible discussion. If the person is being obstinate, stubborn and bull-headed in regard to their sin, mention and discuss with them the reality of Hell in a matter of fact way, but not simply to scare them into submission. Remember Paul's words in 1 Timothy 1:5: "But the goal of our instruction is love from a pure heart and a good conscience and a sincere faith." That's what we're after too.

The goal is always to push people from an obedience based on fear of God to a devotion based on love for God. For that reason, reminders about Hell are necessary, but too many of them will drive the person away, thinking that God is too harsh. We have to exercise wisdom in understanding when to encourage people toward the truth, and when to spur them on to action.

13

Knowing When to Walk Away

It seems counter-evangelistic to say, but there may come a time when we will need to walk away from studying the Gospel with someone. It is a fact that God Himself admitted after centuries of His dealings with the Israelites (2 Kings 17:7-23; Hosea 13:4-11), and Jesus told the Jews after even more rejection of God's Word (Matthew 23:33-39). Paul remarked in Acts 13:46 that the Jews had "judged themselves unworthy of eternal life" and as such, they were now "turning to the Gentiles." He also claimed in 2 Thessalonians 2:11 that those who have already decided to turn from God will be sent a "deluding influence" so that they will "believe what is false," in essence, giving them up to their own desires (Romans 1:26). But perhaps no language is stronger than Jesus' own admonition in the sermon on the mount to not "give what is holy to dogs, and do not throw your pearls before swine" (Matthew 7:6). Is Jesus saying that we should just give up on teaching people the Gospel when it gets "too difficult?"

Like some other statements by Jesus, this one has largely been abused as well, with people "writing off" potential con-verts long before they should. Statements like "they'll never obey the Gospel," or "why am I even wasting my time with him?" pepper conversations that we have with one another, decrying the fact that "no one today will understand the Gospel." But Jesus is hardly advocating a "no-evangelism" mindset; after all, a "perfect" convert has most likely already been converted. Besides, how would you feel if someone wrote you off too soon?

> *The fact that the majority of the people will reject the Gospel should not keep us from trying to reach the ones that will. Only walk away when it is clear that their only interest is in rejecting and defaming God's message.*

Nevertheless, there may come a time when we have to rightly judge an individual's heart, and say to ourselves, "I am (in fact) wasting my time with this person. They neither now, nor will ever, have any desire to obey the Gospel." Making such a decision is hard, as we are, in essence, giving someone up to the desires of their heart, and praying that someone else in the future will have better luck than we do. Because of that, we had better be confident in the decision that we have made.

What Jesus is advocating in Matthew 7 is not an abandonment when the evangelism gets tough, but a wise understanding of what the contact's intentions are; at that point in the discussion(s), you will know them well enough to be able to discern that. Is someone hostile to what you are talking to them about? Try asking questions. Have you run out of things to say? Bring in another person. Do you keep cycling back to the same issue? Examine the discussion again and look for opportunities to expand it. Is it obvious that they only have a "morbid interest in controversial questions" (1 Timothy 6:4)?

Then it might be time to move on to greener pastures, but only after (1) prayer, (2) letting them know you're moving on, and (3) more prayer.

Jesus' interest in Matthew 7 should be the same as ours: preserving the integrity of the Gospel Word. You wouldn't take your fine china and give it to a two-year-old on a sugar rush would you? Then why would you give the Gospel to someone who you know will abuse it? The language is similar to that used in Hebrews 10:29, which described someone who "trampled under foot the Son of God, regarded as unclean the blood of the covenant by which he was sanctified, and insulted the spirit of grace." Harsh words, but fitting given what a beautiful gift salvation is. Everyone is entitled to a fair hearing of the Gospel, but for those who have "judged themselves unworthy of eternal life," they will have to live with their decision. And so will we when we walk away, for better or for worse.

Want to Continue Your Walk With Jesus?

With every book, I take my responsibility to deliver sound Biblical material very seriously, and that extends to the newsletter that is sent out regularly. In it, you will find a short(ish) article that is designed to be encouraging and exhortative, as well as various other materials, such as links to other books you may be interested in - mine and/or others'. These are delivered free of charge and are solely designed to help you draw closer to Him.

PLUS, as an added bonus, I want to give you TWO FREE BOOKS to say thank you:

·Lord, Teach Us to Pray: Learning to Pray Through the Examples in Scripture
·Harmony of the Gospels: Four Books. Eighty-Nine Chapters. One Messiah.

Both of these books are absolutely FREE OF CHARGE just for signing up for my mailing list. Just sign up through this link, and they will be delivered automatically after confirmation (if you do not receive the e-mail, please check your spam).

Again, thank you so much for reading, and I hope to see you again soon!

In Him,
Brady Cook

www.coffeeandaBible.com

Like What You Read?

Hopefully so, but even if you didn't, I would love it if you would head to Amazon and leave a review for this book. Along with letting me know exactly what you did or didn't like, it also provides social proof to others who may be looking for the exact same material. Since I am independently published, I don't have the marketing muscle that goes behind the big conglomerates, so my books live or die based off the reviews people like you give. I also read every single one of them (sometimes compulsively), so rest assured I will hear you loud and clear.

If there's something else you would like me to know, but don't want to leave it in a review, feel free to e-mail me at Brady@CoffeeandaBible.com (or through this link). I love hearing from my readers, no matter if it's good or bad! Thank you again for your support!

Printed in Great Britain
by Amazon